ABDUL RAHMAN

Prospects of Pakistan's Diplomatic Relations

I dedicate this book to great statesman and National Hero –The premier of Islamic Republic of Pakistan , Imran Khan for taking the country of out financial crisis and Reshaping the foreign Policy on the basis of equality and honour .

Abdul Rahman –The Author

Contents

1

Foreign Policy-Past & Present

Pakistan's Foreign Policy has always remained the Arab Centric with Saudi Arab having Central role and Even its alignment towards the US since Independence. Pakistan has never revisited its Foreign Policy holistically to suit the Needs of the country on independent approach.

Since Independence, Pakistan has never clarified its stance on Foreign Policy development and the Terms of Engagement with its neighbours and the big powers. That was why Pakistan's First Prime Minister Liaquat Ali Khan Preferred the US than Russia for its Friendship and paid his visit to America and became the part of West Block than East Block ie the then USSR.

Though Pakistan played a pivotal role in Russia-Afghan war but this strategic partnership did not bear any fruit for the nation due to Political instability, Strong Military Intervention and weak fiscal Policies.

This Diplomatic relationship or bonhomie has never proved Fruitful for the country owing to America being a fair weather Friend as Pak-US relations have always been marred by Distrust. Even Security Aid offered to Pakistan by America affected its

Independent Foreign Policy to the extent that the used aid as pressure tool to force Pakistan to do More to combat terrorism and remove Safe haven of terrorists within Pakistan Domain . Although, Pakistan laid down numerous sacrifices of Soldiers and Civilians; approximately over 100000 in so-called War against Terrorism. Pakistan has already paid a heavy price to be an Ally of Pakistan.

Especially, American led NATO strikes on Afghanistan in which Pakistan was asked to cooperate and hand over the Airports and Roads for Transportation of weapons to Afghanistan for NATO forces to topple Taliban Government and to kill or capture Osama Bin Ladin -The Master Mind of 9/11 Strike on World Trade Centre. American president Bush attacked Afghanistan to avenge the 9/11 incident and to please his fellow Americans. Ever since the Strike, Afghanistan is still unstable despite the passage of 17 years of American led NATO Forces Presence. Even Taliban control 40 % of Afghanistan till today. There is no peace and frequents Suicide attacks on NATO forces and civilians have become the order of the day.

America is losing the Afghan war against terrorism badly but it resorts to blame Pakistan for Terrorist Safe Havens along the Durand line and its fiasco in Afghan War is being associated with Pakistan but the statistics suggest that Pakistan has suffered a lot than the US. Hundreds of Civilians and Soldiers were killed in Suicide Bomb blasts on Mosques, Churches, Temples, Schools and other Political Rallies.

This happened because Pakistan cooperated with the US in Afghanistan allowing it to use Pakistan's soil against Taliban. Such cooperation enraged Taliban against Pakistan and they become fierce enemies of Pakistan – especially its brave Armed forces who initiated their major offensive against these Extremists in shape of Operation Zarb-e-Azb and Operation Rad-ul-Fassad which broke their Waist and Pakistan returned to peace. The Pak-Aghan border became the route for Aghan Taliban to penetrate in KPK and Punjab. Our Political Parties have never mandated the Security agencies against such extremist forces owing to their close linkages with them by a few political parties who have never condemned these elements rather supported them privately. After APS attack, Political parties gave go head to Paramilitary forces to launch Operation after adopting National Action Plan and establishing NACTA.

Pakistan Army has given unprecedented sacrifices for the defence of the country but Americans remained stuck to do more and same narrative of "Do More" prompted American President Donald Trump to blame Pakistan Through tweet that Pakistan has deceived US despite being paid billions in Security Aid. That blame stirred widespread protests against Us in Pakistan by various Parties. Even, ISPR Chief Major General Asif Ghafoor said that the aid they received is just $225 Million, not Billion.Even, the then PML-N Government was on the same page with ISPR and decided to review and reshape their Policy with new and equal terms of Engagement with the US but unfortunately that did not materialize since it was too late for them to respond as there was no Foreign Minister in PML-N Government for almost four years, only Sartaj Aziz worked as Advisor to PM on Foreign Affairs . Pakistan did fail in devising an independent foreign Policy due to being the recipient of Security aid from the US and they stood Mum over the issue for several days until the regular debate on Electronic Media compelled them clarify and respond to the allegation that rocked the country's supremacy and Respect amongst world Nations.

Now, when PTI has emerged as single majority Party at Centre and likely to form government in Center, Punjab, KPK and Coalition Government in Baluchistan, It has great opportunity to devise an independent Foreign Policy for Pakistan to boost up its image Internationally and building Trade ties with neighbours. In his Victory Speech, Imran Khan envisaged his Foreign Policy that he intends to extend trade links and economic connectivity in the region and beyond. In the Foreign Policy of PTI led Government, Saudi Arab and Iran will have central role followed by Old friend China. He resolved to maintain friendly relations with China and continue the CPEC projects for Infrastructural Development of Pakistan. He said that relationship with Saudi Arab and Iran will benefit Pakistan on ideological grounds and help improve Pakistan economically.

He also Envisaged US-Pak Relations on equality basis which may be beneficial for both Nations rather than the imposition over other. Especially, Imran Khan's interests in maintaining Stability in Afghanistan as except this, there would be looming security threats for Pakistan. Pakistan envisages engagement with Washington on equality basis and as a key ally to the US on basis of Mutual interest and trust.

He aspired that there should be peace in Afghanistan so that we have open borders with Afghanistan for trade as Afghanistan is a landlocked Country and it has only option to have traded through Pakistan.

About relations with India, he had the clear position that Pakistan wants Trade with India and other neighbours but the Kashmir issue has the central role. He offered India for dialogue to discuss the issue on Table Talks rather than indulging in Blame Game for Internal incidents. He stressed that the trade between Pakistan and India will mutually benefit both countries. Since PTI's main objective is to revive the Pakistan economy and decrease the growing foreign Debt and boosting and attracting investments in the country. He went on to say that If India advances one Step forward, I would advance two steps as it is very important for the people of Kashmir that the issue must be resolved through Dialogue to pave the way for the trade.

Let's hope that if PTI led Government reshapes the Foreign Policy of Pakistan and the Terms of Engagement with Neighbors and big powers i.e US, China and Russia, it will have far-reaching effects and Pakistan will reap the benefits of Regional Connectivity and revival of Economy provided that the New Envisioned Policy is implemented in letter and spirit. Since it is the right time to do every possible attempt and utilize every possible option to revive the economy and bringing in foreign investments and getting rid of foreign Debt.

Imran Khan's Foreign Policy Vision has been welcomed by the world especially Saudi Arab, Iran, India, US, China and Afghanistan and all the countries showed their resolve to extend bilateral relations with New PTI Government of Pakistan. Even, Afghan President, Ashraf Ghani through his tweet confirmed that he had Telephonic conversation with Imran Khan and have extended the invitation to Imran Khan to pay his kind visit to Afghanistan and reiterated his stance to extend bilateral relations. Similar gesture was also shown by Saudi Arab, Iran, China, US and India through their Ambassadors and foreign Office Spokesmen.

There is also a plan in the ranks of PTI to invite all the SAARC Member Nations" PMs, Presidents including Indian PM Narendra Modi, Afghan President, Ashraf Ghani, Saudi Arab Prince, Turkish President Erdogan to participate in oath taking ceremony of Imran Khan as PM of Pakistan but PTI's spokesman Mehmood-ul Rashid confirmed that such development is in pipeline and it will be discussed in the meeting after the process of formation of Governments in center, Punjab and KP.

2

Opening of Kartarpur Corridor- A Step towards Indo-Pak Peace

With Pakistan and India making history with groundbreaking Ceremony of Kartarpur Corridor on both sides of International Boundary to facilitate the people by giving access to Sikhs of India to Baba Guru Nanak Gurdwara- the founder and spiritual leader of Sikhism. Imran Khan conducted Groundbreaking Ceremony of Kartarpur on 28th November in a huge gathering attended by a delegation from India including Navjot Sidhu.

As an agreement, Pakistan will build a corridor of 4 Kilometer up to International boundary and India will build the same from Gurdaspur to International Boundary of just 2 Kilometers.

Apart from Religious point of view, the corridor will serve a vital role for Trade and Economic relations and improve ties between two hostile Nations for seven decades. The Kartarpur corridor has strategic Importance and can go a long way bringing two countries closer to Diplomatic Dialogue since both countries may turn over a new leaf to build the strong ties and bury the hatchet to spread love and bring peace in the region.

Ever Since Indian Former cricketer Navjot Sidhu Visited Pakistan on the Good Will gesture and bringing in the Message of Peace and Love from India in the Official Invitation from Imran Khan to participate in his oath-taking ceremony, he was warmly welcomed by all including Army Chief General Qamar Jawed Bajwa. Sidhu appeared very optimistic about the Growing friendly ties between the two countries and bringing the message of love and Peace for the people of Pakistan.

The Army chief General Qamar Jawed had a big hug with Sidhu and offered to open the Kartarpur Corridor for the Sikh devotees to visit their founder Baba Guru Nanak Gurdwara by giving visa-free access in order to honour the Guest of honour, Navjot Sidhu. Sidhu was very excited to know that an Army chief had offered such thing as it was really unbelievable for him that an army chief could offer such gesture.

His immediately discussed the matter with the Indian government upon his return to his country. The BJP Government at first turned down the proposal and the so-called Indian Media criticized Navjot Sidhu of Hugging Army chief as India consider him the murderer of His soldiers. There were debates over the television that whether Sidhu should have gone to Pakistan or not.

The Veteran cricketer turned politician Navjot was undeterred and kept pushing Indian Government to accept the Proposal of Kartarpur Corridor. At last, the Modi Government accepted the offer and the foundation Stone Ceremony took place on Indian side on 26th November 2018 by the Vice President of India m Venkaiah Naidu. The Distance from the Indian side is 4 Kilometers from Dera Baba Nanak in India's Gurdaspur District to International Boundary to connect the same with the Gurdwara Kartarpur Sahib in Pakistan.

On the Other hand, The Prime Minister of Pakistan Imran

Khan laid the foundation Stone on 28thNovember 2018 at District Narowal attended by COAS Qamar jawed Bajwa, Navjot Sidhu and Other delegates from India. PM offered Visa Free Access to the Holy site of Durbar Kartarpur Sahib in order to facilitate the Sikh community pilgrims.

According to Vice President of India, "The corridor will become a symbol of love and peace between both countries," Naidu was quoted as saying in Gurdaspur. He went on to say that this was very momentous and historic day and they are fulfilling the wish of Sikh Devotees who are excited to visit the sacred place for Sikhs to celebrate 550th Birthday anniversary of Baba Guru Nanak next year.

Indo-Pak Relations have always remained tense due to various Loc based firing, 26/11 Mumbai Attack and the core issue of Kashmir. There were frequent proposals and demands to have a corridor to facilitate Sikh Pilgrims of India to have access to Gurdwara Baba Guru Nanak so as to perform their religious rituals there.

The Immigration and Visa processes were very exhausting and complicated given the tough hostile relations of these neighbours having fought two deadly wars and frequent cold war that impeded the peace efforts and suspended the mean-ingful dialogue to discuss the grave issues of Terrorism and Kashmir dispute as per the wishes of Kashmiri People through a plebiscite.

The political leadership of both countries have never been engaged in a proper way that might have paved the way to the resolution of issues, Since of there has been a great dearth of Confidence-building measures and trust that might have led both countries to ink an agreement.

Unfortunately, the dialogue process was marred and remained suspended given the growing extremist forces such as Shiv Sina and RSS. The Indian leadership failed to withstand the mounting pressure and consequently, succumbed to pressure and took a U-turn from the dialogue by giving any excuse to justify their distancing from the dialogue process.

However, ever since the PTI-led Government came into power, it reshaped and realigned their foreign policy to suit the interests of the country and defined new terms of engagement with the US and the Neighbours especially Iran, Afghanistan, India and close all-weather friend China.

To break the stalemate and diffuse the tensions between the two countries, the cricket diplomacy came into play when soon after winning the election, Imran Khan envisaged his foreign policy vision inviting India to forward one step and he would go by two steps to reach a lasting solution through dialogue. To display the friendly gesture and using his old cricket fellows of India to bridge the gap and reconnect to Pakistan's intentions to re-initiate the dialogue process, PM Imran Khan invited Navjot Sidhu to attend his oath-taking ceremony.

Sidhu was given warm reception at the ceremony and the big hug from COAS Qamar Jawed Bajwa was the turning point that melted the ice when he(Bajwa) offered to open the Kartarpur Corridor to facilitate the Sikh Pilgrims to visit their Holy place of Guru Nanak Sahib owing to frequent demand. He said to Sidhu to discuss the issue with his Indian Government to make sure whether they were willing or not.

Sidhu was excited and returned home with the proposal but his Indian Government rejected the proposal by giving the traditional excuse of cross-border terrorism and afterwards when Sikh community pushed the Government to accept the proposal. They agreed to build a modern Corridor equipped with all modern facilities on the Indian side and urged Pakistan to build the same from their side.

Pakistan Government welcomed the move and announced groundbreaking ceremony on November 28th and invited Indian Minister for External Affairs Sushma Swaraj, Indian Punjab Chief Minister Amarinder Singh, Congress leader Navjot Singh Sidhu besides 17 Indian journalists to Kartarpur Corridor.

Sushma Swaraj and Chief Minister Punjab Amarinder Singh apologized to come due to some commitments, whereas few Indian Ministers, Journalists and Navjot Sidhu were the part of Indian Delegation came to participate in the groundbreaking ceremony. They termed the development as historic since it would spread the message of love for both countries.

As per the plan, the Indian government will construct and develop the Kartarpur Corridor from Dera Baba Nanak in Indian Punjab's Gurdaspur district to the border, while Pakistan will build the other part of the corridor connecting the border to the Gurdwara in the Kartarpur Sahib area of Narowal district as per the official statement of both countries.

Geographically, the two sites – Dera Baba Nanak and Kartarpur Sahib – are barely separated by six kilometres but parted by an international borderline between India and Pakistan that is also toughened by a poisonous rhetoric and lack of Mutual trust.

It is high time that both countries should make serious efforts to ensure people to people contacts and melt the ice that hampered development in the regions. The Kartarpur Corridor may open vistas of opportunities between two countries and they may take the bilateral trade relations to next level if the same corridor is used for trade besides the purpose of Sikh pilgrims.

It might be too early to predict, yet to be optimistic, the corridor will play its role to diffuse tensions between two countries and may bring the relations to normalization if the priorities and attitudes start changing as people set aside all the odds and need love since they are fed up from the warmongering from Indian Authorities . War would be disastrous for both Nuclear capacious neighbours and will bring misery by plunging country into an economic crisis that will never be fruitful for these countries and for South Asia as a whole.

Pakistan may offer the CPEC partnership if positive and meaningful dialogue process restarts since we have to forward by burying our past differences as quoted by PM Imran Khan during the Groundbreaking ceremony regarding the two European powers France and Germany by saying that if these two can engage in an alliance then why not Pakistan and India Since animosity and wars cannot stand longer if people Start pushing their Governments to maintain peace and live like peaceful neighbours.

.

3

US-PAK Diplomatic Relations Post 9/11 Era

With the changing geo-strategic Situation and after the Twitter blitz, Donald Trump has turned to Pakistan to get rid of the Afghan mess and is seeking help from Islamabad to influence the Taliban by bringing them to the negotiating table. The Russian Peace Talks with the participation of the stakeholders along with Insurgent Taliban leadership and Afghanistan Peace Council Delegation held talks in Moscow to reach an agreement but the talks, unfortunately, did not bear any fruit.

US-Pakistan relations have always been overcast with mis-trust but this time, the onus has been felt and new terms of engagement have surfaced with the New Government of Pakistan. Imran Khan in his exclusive interview with the Washington Post has made it clear that Pakistan is not a hired gun and will not fight anyone's war.

The Peace in Afghanistan is in favour of Pakistan. The Foreign Office will draft a reply to the letter and will present it to Prime Minister Imran Khan for approval. The analysts and political pundits have termed the development as positive, and this time the Trump administration seems to be serious in their engagement with Pakistan. The incoming US central command Lieutenant General Kenneth McKenzie, has also said that he will engage with Pakistan on priority basis as directed by the US president; since the US wants to start direct talks with the insurgent Taliban and bring them to negotiating table to devise a sharable government plan and the possible amendments in the Afghan Constitution.

With Kartarpur Corridor opening to facilitate the Sikh Pilgrims of India and the recent paradigm shift in the US-Pakistan Relations, are being termed as watershed moments for both Pakistan and the US to work together to bring normalcy in Afghanistan. Since both US and Pakistan have suffered a lot in the so-called War on terror and Pakistan has done a lot more than expected as a US Ally.

Pakistan facilitated the US by giving her ground, air and communication channels that played a vital role as a close ally in post 9/11 arena and the US' bid for a regime change in Afghanistan.

Donald Trump's irresponsible Twitter tirade against Pakistan blaming that despite paying millions of Rupees in security aid, Pakistan has deceived the US and did not do a damn thing, has stirred widespread criticism. The global community is well aware that Pakistan suffered a lot being a US ally that is the mistrust that has become a stalemate between US-Pak relations, and the ambiguities that have stalled the diplomatic relations.

Pakistan facilitated the US by giving her ground, air and communication channels that played a vital role as a close ally in post 9/11 arena and the US' bid for a regime change in Afghanistan

With increasing US alignment towards India and signing various trade agreement with the Modi Regime, they have also created a sense of disappointment in the circles of civil and military leadership of Pakistan that despite using us as a scapegoat and a hired gun — our arch rivals are being favoured.

The US might have been advised by various think-tanks and Influencing bodies of political and diplomatic circles that an ally who fought the war on terror is an important ally of the US, however, still Pakistan's sacrifices are sidelined.

Instead of giving support, the US withheld a huge chunk of security aid and even tried to influence the International Monetary Fund (IMF) not to offer any bailout packages, as it may be used to repay Chinese loans.

Moreover, the US has always demanded that Pakistan do more, and that is really disappointing. Despite all these odds, Pakistan's civil and military leadership appears to be on the same page and ready to engage with the US on revised terms of engagement for the sake of peace.

Both Pakistan and the US have suffered losses, now, it is time that they should serve the common interests of each other. Pakistan can play a key role in the Afghan peace process since this time, the regional powers of Asia such as Russia, China, India, Pakistan, Turkey and US intend to resolve the issue through dialogue as the Americans have failed to bring peace despite their presence in Afghanistan for the last 17 years.

This is perhaps one of the longest wars they have fought and apparently, they are losing ground since the Taliban seem to be much organized and have become a party to talk too rather than an insurgent group. They have control of various provinces and possess great influence in their controlled areas.

The Afghan Peace process will never succeed unless all the stakeholders are on board especially the Taliban leadership, as prior to the US–led Air strikes, Taliban had full control of all the areas of Afghanistan.

Owing to being a landlocked country, Afghanistan depends on Pakistan for trade and supplies. The Peace Process may pave the way for Pakistan-Afghanistan Transit Trade Agreement (APTTA) that was a bilateral trade agreement signed in 2010 that calls for greater facilitation in the movement of goods between these two countries.

The China Pakistan Economic Corridor is yet another trade route that will benefit Afghanistan if is peace agreement reached between the Taliban and the Afghan Government.

CPEC is a game changer not only for Pakistan but also for the Central Asian States. The analysts are of the view that CPEC may trigger a Hybrid war since it has a very significant geostrategic position that will attract more countries towards it, including the OPEC to use the Gwadar Port for transportation of Oil and LPG gas to the South Asian and Central Asian States.

It is imperative that Pakistan and the US work together for regional peace and especially to reach an agreement with the insurgent Taliban leadership so that Peace can be maintained and restored in Afghanistan.

The withdrawal plan for NATO forces may be chalked out and the refugees' crisis may be overcome, since Pakistan has not been compensated despite being overburdened by 1.45 million Afghan Refugees as per the recent statistics of UNHCR. Furthermore, the UNHCR termed Pakistan as the world's biggest country to host such high number of Refugees.

It is hoped that this change of attitude will benefit both the countries, and will improve diplomatic relations and will help in finding lasting solutions to bring peace in the war-torn Afghanistan and the repatriation of Afghan refugees.

4

A Robust Change in Foreign Policy

The robust change in foreign policy has started bearing fruit for Pakistan since the countries like the US and Russia have appreciated Pakistan's role in peace process as well as in the War on Terror.

The World has started to appreciate the positive image projected by PTI Government under PM Khan. Undoubtedly, a new chapter of peaceful Pakistan has unfolded where the peace has a central role to play.

The opening of Kartarpur Corridor, peace efforts for Afghanistan quagmire and propagating peaceful settlement for Indian-Occupied Kashmir (IOK) on the basis of UN resolutions will certainly bear fruit and carve the way of progress and economic boom for crisis-ridden Pakistan.

Luckily, the diplomatic relations in the existing circumstances have been very effective due to PTI's effective implementation of external policy to engage with world powers including the all-weather friend China. The Prime Minister's visits to Saudi Arabia, China, UAE and Turkey have painted a positive image of Pakistan Globally and even in his poll victory speech had drawn the attention of the world that Pakistan intends to enjoy friendly and peaceful relations with the world especially China, Iran, Afghanistan, Russia, Saudi Arabia, Turkey, US, Central Asian States, the Middle and the Far East .

> *The opening of Kartarpur Corridor, peace efforts for Afghanistan quagmire and propagating peaceful settle-ment for Indian-Occupied Kashmir on the basis of UN resolutions will certainly bear fruit and carve the way of progress and economic boom for crisis-ridden Pakistan*

Imran Khan's speech was also welcomed by India since he had offered India to initiate strategic dialogue to restart the stalled talks. He went on to say that if India comes forward one step he will advance twice.

Pakistan's Foreign Minister Shah Mehmood Qureshi has so far played the instrumental role by visiting the Kabul and holding a meeting with President Ashraf Ghani to ensure Pakistani role in peacebuilding process especially the US phased withdrawal plan and influencing the Taliban to come to negotiating table.

With Russia taking lead in hosting the Afghan Taliban moot after almost 30 Years of Afghan invasion with an aim to find a peaceful political solution to the Afghan mess. Historically, the Soviet Union disintegrated after sustaining a humiliating defeat at the hands of the Afghan Mujahedeen and insurgent groups.

It is like history repeating itself since unlike Russia, the US plans to initiate the phased withdrawal. The US has fought the longest war ever in Afghanistan but consequently lost the war morally that prompted it to pull its forces out of Afghanistan in phases so that civil administration may take the charge of security.

The US intention for regime change was half fulfilled in terms of toppling the Taliban regime but it has not been able to suppress or weaken the insurgent Taliban rather they have become little stronger and controlling vast areas.

That was the reason that after his twitter tirade against Pakistan, Donald Trump changed its aggressive stance against Pakistan and wrote a letter to PM Khan for help to bring peace in war-torn Afghanistan. That is really a tragic and dismal end to US-Afghan war since the US mission remained impossible due to strong Taliban. Trump Administration followed aggressive policies that led them to isolation.

In this connection, two sessions of talks were held. The first round of talks was hosted by Russia in Moscow and the second was held in UAE with Taliban Leadership.

Pakistan will keep on playing its role for peace in Afghanistan since it's in best interests of the country to secure its borders especially the trade routes of CPEC. Pakistan's surging balance of payments issue was resolved with the assistance of Saudi Arabia, the UAE and China which is the result of the robust reshaping of foreign policy making it independent based on equality.

Pakistan's recrafted and redesigned foreign policy serves its interest in the best manner and all credit goes to PM Imran Khan, Foreign Minister Shah Mehmood Qureshi and his Foreign Office team for projecting the positive image of Pakistan in the world. This positive image will attract more foreign investment in the country since apart from external policy, the internal policy has also improved manifold and so far no great incident of terrorism has surfaced thanks to our brave soldiers of the Rangers, Army and the Police who are always ready to sacrifice their lives to defend the dear homeland with true spirit of Patriotism.

5

Pakistan's Role in Emerging New World Order

The changing geostrategic Situation warrants that Pakistan must align its Foreign Policy suiting its national interests so that the soft image of Pakistan could be projected worldwide.

So far, Pakistan has done a tremendous job in projecting the positive image and the world including Pakistan's old ally the US has realized that without Pakistan's help, it cannot get rid of the Afghan conflict; and it is considering the political solution to the Afghan mess since war tactics have failed miserably given the unstable circumstances of law and order in Afghanistan despite the passage of 17 years of War on terror for so-called quest for regime change.

With the changing world order going from bipolar to multi-polar, it could be estimated that After US, Russia, UK, Germany, France, Italy, the new strong powers are born such as the Asian tiger China who have taken the world with great.

On the other hand, the China Pakistan Economic Corridor (CPEC) has also created a possibility of hybrid war since it is aimed at bringing the economic boom in Pakistan by creating a road and rail network,; Coal powered Energy Projects, Hydel and Energy projects and solar energy projects.

The recent activism of Russia and China playing the role for talks with Taliban has borne fruit and Pakistan played a meaningful and constructive role in bringing the Afghan Taliban to the negotiating table and paved the way for US withdrawal.

The Multipolar status of the world has weakened the world powers and has changed their behaviours from aggressiveness to defensiveness or passiveness.

Furthermore, if we analyze the role of past Super Powers i.e the Soviet Union a, we know that it has helped in use of chemical weapons in Syria and the crisis has become very serious since the civilians were targeted that resulted in the loss of civilian lives and destruction of Infrastructure and houses of the people. Even, Russia had also tried to impose its hegemony in Ukraine .

It is arguable that how China and Russia may justify this new world order where Americans still mistakenly consider this world as unipolar and continue their influential and aggressive role unabated. The collapse of the Soviet Union might have created the possibility of a multipolar world with more superpowers making their entry into the power pool despite the existence of earlier players.

The great nations cannot impose their hegemonic doctrines on the basis of military might or economic boom or high GDP growth but they set examples for the world nations to follow.

The great nations inspire the world with their development, not oppression and repression. Great nations like Japan, Malaysia, Indonesia and Singapore have achieved their recognition through innovative education systems and knowledge-driven Economy.

Pakistan's soft image has been appreciated across the globe, especially by regional players like Russia, Iran, Saudi Arabia, China

But regrettably, the British and The US have carried aggressive and oppressive policies towards the world nations that is why they are facing isolation in the world. The British exit from the Eurozone has crippled its economy owing to repeated failures in the Brexit Deal.

On the contrary, Pakistan has done a lot than expected since Pakistan has conducted various Military Operations against the so-called Taliban, militants and terrorists. Pakistan is already under the heavy influx of Afghan refugees that have affected the law and order situation in Pakistan and economy, especially in Karachi the situation has become worse due to criminal activities of these Afghan refugees.

Despite having the longest border with Afghanistan, it is very difficult to monitor the border and beefing up the security arrangements. Several Pakistani soldiers lost their lives due to suicide blasts during checking of the suspected people entering Pakistani territory.

The US ties with Saudi Arabia are also getting tense after the death of Washington Post Saudi columnist Jamal Khashoggi in the Saudi consulate in Istanbul, Turkey.

After much aggression, it is apparent the US wouldn't like to distance itself from Saudi Arabia on this issue.

On the other hand, China an emerging and influential player in the new world order has already done the spadework and has implemented its BRI (Belt and Road Initiative) which also includes multibillion CPEC Project in Pakistan and despite rising pressure and opposition from the US, China's Belt and Road

Initiative is probably not going to be affected.

The multipolarity of the world has forced US president Donald Trump to change his stance and engage with Pakistan to bring Taliban insurgent groups to the negotiating table and bringing peace in Afghanistan since US's phased withdrawal is linked with the successful dialogue with Taliban and reaching possible agreement to get rid of the Afghan stalemate.

Pakistan's present PTI government takes the credit of having crafted and reshaped foreign policy that has already started bearing fruit and Pakistan's soft image globally has been appreciated by the world especially Afghanistan, Russia, Iran, Saudi Arabia, Turkey, British, China, US, Russia and others.

The World has appreciated the countless sacrifices laid down by the valiant soldiers and civilians. Pakistan has already done more; it is up to the US and others to do the same since Pakistan's economy has been crippled due to constantly fighting War on Terror. Pakistan's positive gesture towards normalization of relations with India after the opening of the Kartarpur corridor has projected soft image worldwide.

6

Pakistan's Peace Gestures & India's War-mongering

The relationship between two arch-rivals –India and Pakistan, has never been sound since Independence from British Yoke in 1947. Both countries have fought wars and Pakistan has paid a heavy price after the falling of Dhaka (East Pakistan –Bangladesh) due to the conspiracy of India. India, being the biggest democracy, has always escalated the situation with hegemonic designs and abruptly starts building war hysteria to secure votes in the Elections especially,the sitting PM Narendra Modi whose main grudge lies with Muslims as he had done a similar mess in Gujarat which caused riots resulting in the loss of lives of the Innocent Muslims.

Unfortunately, he was the Chief Minister of Gujarat and all happened due to his propagation of anti-muslim policies and instigating hatred among the Hindus against the Muslims over slaughtering of Cows.

Though he has been elevated to the post of Prime Minister, yet his hate-filled speeches instigated the Indians against Pakistan in post-Pulwama Attack that resulted in causalities of 45 Indian

Armed forces in J&K.

Like the past Practices, without thinking a moment, India started pointed fingers on Pakistan for the said incident by portraying Pakistan, their biggest enemy, though Pakistan's sensible leadership under Imran Khan categorically rejected the Indian Claims considered them baseless.

Imran Khan also offered India to Investigate the matter by the provision of solid evidence. On the contrary, the Indian stubbornness led to Indian aggression when two IAF Jets dropped payloads in haste when PAF Planes pushed them back.

Modi, for face-saving, claimed to have targeted the JeM camps but DG ISPR Major General Scrapped the claims through his tweet with actual pictures where payloads were dropped by IAF jets in haste to escape PAF response.

In a defensive move, Pakistan Air force and Pak Army shot down two IAF jets of India.Even, the forces captured Indian Pilot Wing commander Abhinandan alive who was later released as peace gesture after the decision of the joint session of Parliament.

The world welcomed the move aimed at de-escalation but so called Indian Media, as usual, started portraying and celebrating the peace gesture as their victory which invited wrath and criticism from peace lovers and analysts. While some sensible Journalists even termed it the moral victory of Pakistan that won hearts of the Parents of captured Pilot and put water on the evil designs of PM Modi whose plan failed miserably within days of execution and Pakistan appeared victorious on Diplomatic front internationally and Kashmir Issue came in the limelight

According to various Security experts, There is no possibility of full-scale war as both Neighbours are nuclear powers and the war will have adverse repercussions, not only on both countries but it will engulf the entire region.It might bring miseryan destruction in the region, they feared.

The defence experts are also of the view that the current escalation and the war hysteria built by Modi in order to win election
support from the People of India for his second term as PM
will not happen. As, at the moment, his opposition alliance
seems to be well prepared and will give BJP tough time in all
the states since Indian National Congress Leader Rahul Gandhi
appears to be the most favourite candidate for PM Slot who
enjoys massive support from other opposition parties to form
future Government.

To maintain deterrence and balance of power, to silence the
critics, in a defensive move, Pakistan shot down two IAF jets
and captured wing commander Abhor Nandan alive.

The arrest of Pilot startled belligerent India. Kudos to Pakistan
PM Imran Khan for taking the sensible decision and announcing
the release of the captured pilot for peace gesture while speaking
to the joint session of parliament that sent peace waves to India
and the world.

The World community hailed the decision including US President Donald Trump, UN chief, China, Turkey and Saudi Arabia.

Imran Khan said that if peace returns to both countries with
this move, we are ready to release Abhinandan for the sake of
peace and goodwill.let's live with peace and let the people live
in a peaceful manner.

The senior journalists in India applauded the decision and
welcomed the peace gesture and expected the same from India
but India crossed all the limits of Human rights and stoned to
death an innocent prisoner who had crossed Loc by mistake in
sheer frustration.

Shakirullah became the soft target of Indian war hysteria created
by Narendra Modi and was brutally killed stoning to death by

27

prisoners for so-called revenge.

India still fuelling the war hype through irresponsible News Channels and levelled scores of allegations against Pakistan such as cross border terrorism.

Even, India justified the attack by saying that it was offensive against the terrorists' camp of Jaish e Mohammad. But Indian white lies proved wrong when DG ISPR Major General Asif Ghafoor categorically rejected the Indian claims and posted the pictures of Indian payload that was dropped in haste in the midnight causing no causality.

The DG ISPR Major General Asif Ghafoor's tweet sent tremors which jolted BJP propaganda but the so-called Indian Media even took the peace gesture as weakness and started calling Abhinandan a hero.

The Peace loving and optimist journalists criticized the irresponsible reporting of Indian Media and called for immediate halt to such war Mongering and spreading hatred through Media including social media channels while Pakistani media presented the true picture and displayed responsibility understanding the gravity of the issue.

The Senior leaders of Indian National Congress and other opposition parties started protesting against Modi's warmongering and demanded immediate halt to such anti-peace initiative aimed at winning political support for upcoming Indian General Elections which will decide the fate of BJP and Other Parties to determine as who is going to be crowned as Next Prime Minister of India.

Modi's Premiership sickness has no bounds and he is playing with fire in a dangerous game of War that might bring misery not only for belligerent neighbours but will engulf the whole region. Even it might be disastrous for the entire world if nuclear weapons were used.

Modi's abortive efforts to win the elections at the cost of risking Peace, will never be fulfilled since Wars bring misery, hunger, disease and destruction in the world given the alarming repercussions of World war-I and World War –II and loss of millions of innocent lives in the quest of Power, egoism and supremacy for some vested interests and endangering the whole nation at the cost of small gains.

It is not a sensible decision to push the country on the back-burner and destroy economic opportunities with belligerent behaviour.

Though the offer of mediation from US president Donald Trump was turned down by India, but Luckily, despite Indian warmongering, Pakistan has achieved tremendous diplomatic support at apex forums when UN Chief, US, Russia, Turkey and OIC member countries and Kashmir seem to be slipping from the hand of India.

The issue has been raised by Foreign Minister Shah Mehmood Qureshi at Diplomatic level that has started bearing fruit for Pakistan in terms of Moral Support whereas India has been heavily criticized and condemned at all levels.The UN Secretary General Antonio Guterres has offered his office for mediation between Two Neighbours to deescalate the Situation.

In short, Pakistan is fortunate enough to have professional Armed forces whose professional attitude was lauded by Indian Pilot Abhinandan during the detention period.

In his video message, he appreciated the professional behaviour of Pakistan Army and lambasted Indian Media for Warmongering and Fake News.

He further said that he was treated in a fair manner and even Armed Forces saved him from the people who were beating him.

Such a video was a slap on the face of Modi and his all cards and tactics failed miserably and ended tragically. Thus, Pakistan has won the battle morally and peacefully.

Pakistan's befitting response terrified India which prompted the Foreign Minister Sushma Swaraj to hold the press conference and declared that they want peace and not war. Pakistan welcomed the statement decision and reaffirmed resolve to demonstrate the same.

Furthermore, Indian aggression also brought both PTI led Government and opposition parties on the same page and they extended their full support to Armed Forces and Military leadership.

The captive Indian Pilot Abhinandan was released as per announcement and handed over to Indian Forces while Pakistan received stone riddled dead body of Prisoner Shakirullah in return.

Pakistan has offered India hundred times to initiate the strategic dialogue to get rid of Stalemate but India has always tried to avoid the dialogue process and speeded up atrocities in Jammu& Kashmir and Indian Killing spree seems to have no limits.

The mass scale use of chemical weapons and pelt guns calls for the intervention of the World community especially UN to urge India to demilitarize J&K and start the dialogue process.

Since the 17-year long US war in Afghanistan has failed to give desired results and India must learn a lesson from it and refrain from further escalation of war like situation rather the efforts should be made for normalization of Relations so that trade relations and people to people contact may be restored in mutual interest.

Pakistan has always remained calm and Patient demonstrated willingness and readiness to talks but India never engaged with

Pakistan for meaningful dialogue and often walks away owing to internal pressure.

The dynamic Pakistani leadership has demonstrated the show of patience and forbearance, though PM Imran Khan had authorized the Army forces to retaliate if War is imposed upon Pakistan.

It is hoped that both the neighbours will sit together and address their issues through dialogue rather than creating a war like situation that has already ensured their stock Exchange Point losses due to war clouds and uncertainty.

We should also give credit to our valiant Forces especially Pakistan Army and Pakistan Air force acting on time and defending the frontiers of Motherland.

We are really proud of our forces and the PTI led Government especially Army chief Qamar Javed Bajwa and PM Imran Khan by showing tolerance and bearing the pressure boldly and making the nation proud and at the same time promoting love and peace as Peace opens the countless opportunities for development and Progress.

Let's hope that both countries should jointly wage a war against terrorism and Poverty and should live like good neighbours and settle their disputes in a friendly environment through meaningful dialogue.

7

Possible US Withdrawal and Afghan Peace

The Afghan soil has been very difficult for the invaders whoever tried to occupy it or tried to impose their hegemonic rule. Everybody is well aware that what happened with the two big powers i.e US and the then Soviet Union who invaded this Tribal influenced country having sustained heavy losses in terms of armed forces and financial losses.

Afghanis have sustained several insurgencies either religious extremism or communism and having resisted to these forces by fighting guerrilla wars or civil wars. The turbulent nature of circumstances has never been conducive for any foreign invaders.

Pakistan being key US ally has paid a heavy price since thousands of the valiant Pakistani soldiers and the innocent civilians have lost their precious lives in the war on terror.

The Soviet Union installed the communist party in a bid to enlarge or expand the communist empire to

Afghanistan. Though, the communist regime in Afghanistan carried out various radicalized thoughts and reformed the constitution on the basis of Communist believes and even tried to suppress the dissent voices through force but such tactics did not bear any fruit and when the Soviet-Afghan war started, the Soviet Union faced utter humiliation in the hands of Insurgent Mujahideen supported by the US and other pro mujahedeen forces .

The Soviet-Afghan war lasted over nine years but given the geostrategic and geographic location of Afghanistan, the Soviet fought an unwinnable war based on furthering the communist thought and bringing the territory in its occupation.

On the contrary, the resistant Afghan and Non-Afghan forces propelled Soviet troops to pull out of Afghanistan as Gorilla war incurred mammoth trouncing to Troops. The Afghans, historically, are the born warriors and that is why they have maintained their freedom for many years. The Soviet Pullout from Afghanistan had left the fragile and weak Civil Government in turmoil and the state witnessed turbulence and chaos after Soviet withdrawal.

The Soviet invasion led to the disintegration of Soviet Union when 15 of States declared independence, thus Afghan soil proved graveyard for the Soviet Union. The US support to the insurgent mujahedeen and other groups had forced Soviet troops to retreat.

likewise ,when US-led NATO forces had entered Afghanistan for the regime change and to nab the most wanted terrorist (in the eyes of US) –Osama-Bin-Laden, The Russia had reportedly extended the Olive branch to insurgent Taliban and had supplied the sophisticated weapons since it was not just war between the insurgent Afghan Taliban and US, but it was war between the two Big powers of past and present –i.e the US and Russia.

To counter, the Twitter blitz, Pakistan government
under PM Khan set the records straight and went on
to say that We are no more hired gun as we have done
a lot and it is US' turn to do more.

Despite battling the longest war and the existence of thousands of US forces in Afghanistan, US has failed to bring peace in Afghanistan and has not been able to suppress the Taliban and retrieve areas from the Afghan Taliban stronghold.

Ironically, the US failure has always been linked to Pakistan and this blame game exists for the years. Pakistan is always pressed to do more despite doing more in so-called the war on terror. Pakistan being key US ally has paid a heavy price since thousands of the valiant Pakistani soldiers and the innocent civilians have lost their precious lives in the war on terror. Despite such unprecedented sacrifices we are still asked to do more and the blame of US failure is associated with Pakistan to hide their weaknesses and humiliating defeat.

Pakistan Armed forces conducted two massive operations namely Zarb-e-Azab and Radul Fasad against terrorists, additionally, targeted operation in Karachi and in some parts Baluchistan where RAW supports the separatist movements. The arrest of in-service Indian Naval Agent Kalbhushan Yadav was the prime evidence Indian involved in Baluchistan when he (Kalbhushan) publicly confessed that he was sent to bring instability in Pakistan and to support the Baloch separatist groups to carry out terrorist activities in the country.

Pakistan is amongst the few countries that have witnessed the heavy influx of refugees after US invasion over Afghan. Thousands of Afghan refugees entered Pakistan through Durand line and settled in KP, Quetta, and Karachi. Even, most of the refugees are not registered at UNHCR camps.

Some of the refugees went to India and Iran as well but the major influx remained in Pakistan reached the number of 1.4 million as per UNHCR report and Pakistan was ranked the country with the highest number of refugees in the world and have been mitigating the refugee crisis on its own since the US has not supported economically. Rather, US president Donald Trump questioned Pakistan that it has not done the damn thing for the US despite payment of millions in US security AID through the much-criticized Twitter tweet and levelled the charges of deception against Pakistan.

To counter, the Twitter blitz, Pakistan government under PM Khan set the records straight and went on to say that We are no more hired gun as we have done a lot and it is US' turn to do more.

> Will the existing Ashraf Ghani Government will survive the US withdrawal if any truce reaches between the Taliban Groups and Afghan government under the power-sharing formula or coalition government.

Donald Trump after the humiliating defeat in US midterm

Elections 2018 and after advice from think tanks, took a U-turn and wrote a letter to a letter to PM Imran Khan seeking help to resolve Afghan conundrum and bringing the insurgent Taliban to the negotiating the table.

The move was welcomed by both Civil and military leadership. Pakistan continued its resolve to play the role for the Afghan peace process. With two rounds of talks; one in Kremlin Moscow hosted by Russia and second in UAE, has proved the possibility of talks and as per the demand of Taliban leadership, US has announced to pull its forces stationed in Afghanistan.

Now, the question arises that how the US will leave the fragile and weak Afghan Government and plans to withdraw its forces stationed at Afghan soil for 17 years. Will the existing Ashraf Ghani Government will survive the US withdrawal if any truce reaches between the Taliban Groups and Afghan government under the power-sharing formula or coalition government.

It is too early to predict but given the prevalent chaotic circumstances, it could be ascertained that the weak Ashraf Ghani government is incapable to cope with the security and economic challenges currently faced by a war-ravaged country where uncertainty surrounds all the hopes of Peace and the 17-year war has brought the misery in Afghanistan.

The US intervention in Afghanistan was aimed at expulsion and eradication of the insurgent groups both Afghan and Non-afghan including the strong resistance force of Taliban having shown their resistance for the last 17 years and the US is the verge of facing yet another humiliating defeat in the hands of Taliban whom it considered the extremist insurgent group and killed thousands of Taliban, now initiated the dialogue process with the same group shows that the US has miserably lost the toughest Unwinnable war on terror in Afghanistan and failed to bring peace and cleanse the so-called terrorists from the Afghan soil.

> It is hoped that Pakistan's efforts for peace will be appreciated by the international community along with Pakistan's role as a close ally of US in War on Terror.

Though it has been able to install US-backed Government as the Soviet Union had done, it has missed the targets and goals set for the longest war it had fought, regrettably, ending in a very disappointing note. It could be said that Trump's Afghan policy has experienced a significant shift after it feared isolation from the world in the Multipolar world order.

Pakistan's stance on finding the political solution to the Afghan imbroglio was finally accepted and Pakistan's new PTI government has reshaped and realigned the priorities in the foreign policy making it very robust to suit its needs in Multipolar world order especially furthering the game changer Project CPEC that has already ignited a hybrid war among the regional players i.e Iran, India, and International player America .

Finally, if the tripartite talks between the US, the Afghan government and the Taliban succeed with support from Pakistan, these will play a pivot role in bringing peace in region and will definitely secure CPEC from hybrid warfare since Afghanistan will also be the key beneficiary owing to its landlocked status and mostly depends on Pakistan for its transit trade.

It is hoped that Pakistan's efforts for peace will be appreciated by the international community along with Pakistan's role as a close ally of US in War on Terror.